# OIL & WATER

# OIL & WATER

*A collection of poetry by*

## Caitlynn Samuel

Illustrations by Laura Samuel

# Acknowledgements


To those who love too much,
never change.
I fell in love all over again putting
this book together and I hope your
heart thinks of someone special every
time you read these. Take that chance
and grow from what happens.

To the two very important people in
my life that encouraged me to share
words with the world.
You're both still here, wow.
Sometimes I can't figure out why
after all we've been through, but I'm
so incredibly thankful for your
patience, your love,
and your encouragement.
To two truly incredible and deserving
souls, from the depths of my heart
and soul I want to thank you both.
I love you.

*"We're like Oil and Water"*, you said.

Back then, the negative implications of this statement hit my chest like a ton of bricks. We know there's no way to mix; we are polar opposites and I admit at times I've been really fucking dense. Yet here we are, after a long year still swirling around each other attempting to make this love work. Lying here thinking of you, I think I finally realized that mixing you and I is not required.
We are two separate substances so vastly different and unique and not commonly found together; we lead two separate and different lives. There's no need to dissolve into one when being an individual is so important. We can coexist next to each other, touching, remaining close and in contact and fulfill exactly what we need together.

I love that about us.

I'm hoping you'll be
the last cup of coffee
to ever burn my lips.
I've learned to handle you
with care and proceed
with caution because
you're much too addicting
to give up.

Paint me with the colors of autumn,
vibrant oranges, yellows, and reds.
This was the season we met and
we've seen many autumns pass since,
together.

And I knew it was you
when the smallest things
started to become the
biggest parts of me.

Settling for
a watered down
version of yourself,
of life,
is a crime because
there are people
who would love to
drown in everything
that you are.

Play these heartstrings like a
song you've written yourself
and I'll follow wherever this life
may lead us, like a lovesick child
entranced by the Pied Piper's sound.

I fell in love
with her sense of adventure,
her maddening beauty,
and the passion in her voice.
When she speaks of her dreams
and the mountains she is
determined to conquer,
I know for certain
that anything is possible.

I try to think of love
like a campfire you've built for survival.
You start your search for the right kindling
and light it carefully; transferring the flame
slowly, cautiously so it won't go out.
It starts to burn and spring to life.
Everyday the fire needs tending; some days may
require more effort or more care than other days.
You may end up with bruises, blisters, scars
from your labor. There will be storms that come,
spring showers and hurricanes will try to put
out the flames you've worked hard to keep alive.
You'll have to put in the work to protect and
nurse that flame through the rain and wind,
ensuring it doesn't go out. If you can weather
the storms, over time you'll learn to construct
a shelter, something stronger to protect what is
important to you. Tending the fire will become
second nature and you'll fall into the smooth
rhythm of life. Although there's always work to
be done, the comfort and warmth of this fire was
all it took to build it up strong.

I want your mouth to
be so full of my name
I can taste it when
I kiss your lips,
and just for a heartbeat,
everything is perfect.

You're guiding me towards home
like the beacon of a lighthouse.
I'll wait out here for your direction,
idling in the open sea,
until you give me the all clear.
Please keep me safe,
I don't think my heart could take
a collision with your rocky shores.

I imagine others must be jealous of
the way you take my hand and shine
so much light through my darkest days.
They envy how I've turned you
into countless poems that have only
gotten better over time, just as we have.
You've shown me the way and, in return,
I've made you my muse.

Our souls understand each other
as if they were never strangers.
Is that why you felt so familiar
back then and still to this day,
no matter the time in between?

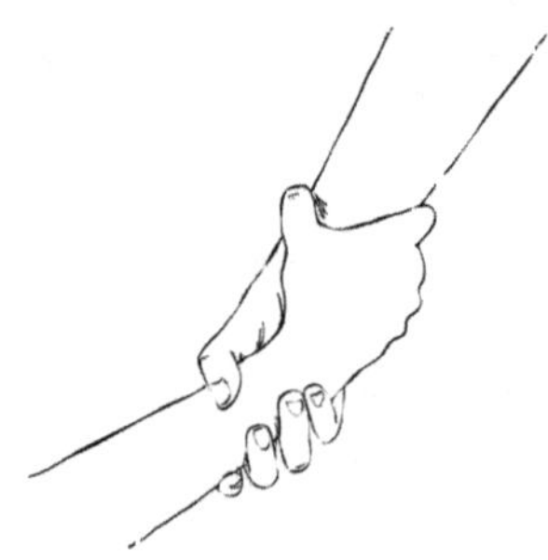

Summer collapses into Fall again
and, after all this time passing,
your touch still makes my pulse react.

The lyrics of the songs she sends
when I cross her wandering mind
are airdropped directly into my veins
and get me so incredibly high
settling the withdrawals I have
been having from her presence,
even if it is just temporary relief.

I couldn't look away if I tried.
You're sinking into my soul and
I've stopped trying to keep control
of all the feelings that surround us.

I need you
like plants need sunlight
to grow, flourish, and survive.

Your voice drips
like pure honey
from your lips
when you sing.

As we lay together outside
just like we did years ago
staring up at the night sky,
a familiar feeling washes over.
You and I, bathed in moonlight like an
unspoken blessing from the Universe.
Under the stars like this with you
it's so easy to understand that we're
a part of something much bigger,
something preplanned and
set in motion once more.

We have become so much closer by
building this foundation together.
I've been slowly, cautiously releasing
pieces of my heart for you to hold onto.
I finally let go of the last piece on
the night you tasted my love for you.
I'm ready to accept the risk that
they might not make it back to me
in the same condition, if at all.
Because there will always be pieces
of me that fully belong to you.
You kept some nine years ago it seems and
the embers never stopped smoldering.

I have my memories
and this tattoo.
I'll choose to look and
remember the good
that was me and you.

Sundays in this house are days of worship.
When our bodies collide in bed
something so holy happens,
I gladly fall to my knees in front of you.
I sing hymns of praise with my tongue
from your neck down to the
temple nestled between your legs.
We don't worship religion in this house,
I pray to the shrine I've dedicated to your
beautiful soul and gladly commit these sins.

Don't run.
I'll keep carrying you
beneath my skin and
write you into my life story.

She is art in the purest form;
pencil lines,
brush strokes,
paint smudges,
and a little hard work.
She is a masterpiece in your eyes;
something to be appreciated,
priceless and
extraordinarily beautiful.

She drives me to
the brink of madness
with those eyes
that shine like stars
and a smile that can
light up the darkest night.

Some days I'd like to
turn back the clock.
I'd chase after you
instead of letting you run,
better yet, I'd find you sooner
and love you completely.

Wrap your hands around my heart
and caress my emotions softly.
Put your lips on my body
and kiss every secret.
Lock eyes with me and
take a photograph of my soul
so you never forget what is
yours to return home to.
Pieces of you have existed in me
for many, many years now
and I don't envision them leaving
anytime soon.

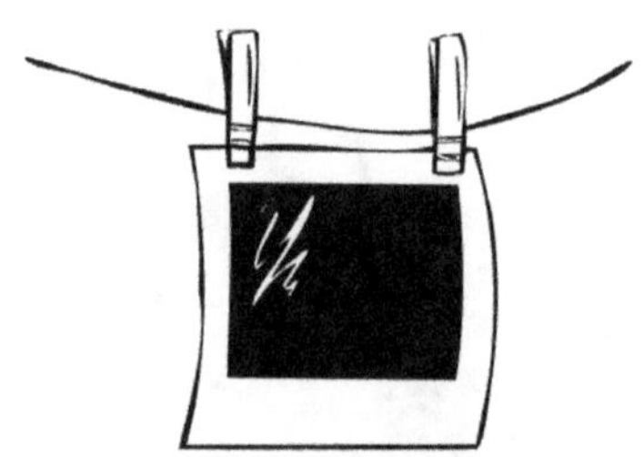

I'll never be too busy to miss you,
you consume my mind and
traverse my thoughts constantly.
No distraction is enough
to make my heart forget
how your touch makes me feel.

I've got these feelings large enough
to fill the galaxy we are a part of.
You and I are a constellation,
connected but nameless for now.
We have yet to be discovered,
to be gazed upon in the night sky,
but when I gaze at you
I'm light-years away in my mind
dreaming of the possibilities
and admiring how stunningly bright
and beautiful a single star can be
when they have found their match.

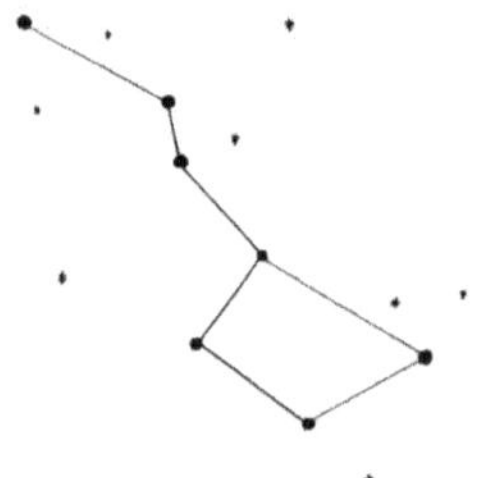

One day at a time
is fine by me,
as long as
those days are
with you.

The feelings I get when
you're wrapped up in my arms
with our fingers interlocked
and my heart beating too fast
while I listen to your breathing
and feel the weight of your body
and soul on top of mine
can never be put into words.
I can tell you, however,
that this is where you belong
and it's these arms that will
never fail to keep you safe.

I know I hold your hand
a little too tight most days,
but I want you to love me
for a lifetime.
So I'll love you
like it's the only act
I know and if somehow
this comes to an end,
I'll know I've tried my hardest
to etch you into my soul,
if only you'd given me the chance.

You'll never find the need to
second guess my feelings for you.
I wear my heart on my sleeve
to a goddamn fault.

I've been trying to figure out why I write;
to help with an emotional release,
to keep my mental health under control,
and to empty you from my mind or is it
to make sure I can never forget you.
I think these words are meant for you in a way,
they've never flowed so freely across
my pages for anyone else before.
If someone else discovered them
they wouldn't truly comprehend the meaning.
I can't seem to speak words as
well as I can write them, but,
I want to make sure you know
how much one person can love you.

Describe your fantasies to me in detail
so I can make them come true.
I want to taste everything you're made of,
all the different parts of you.

The beat draws us in
dancing together as
our bodies start to touch.
This song will always mean
something special to me but
you are the lyrics I can't seem
to get out of my head.

Being with you feels so effortless,
like the way the waves kiss the shore
as if there's no force urging them forward.
You and I have nothing propelling us on,
maybe that's why you keep slipping
through my fingers like sand.

I'm trying to be quiet
even though my soul
is begging me to
show you the way home.
I must teach it patience.

I am tethered
to you in ways
I cannot explain.

Let me love the
lonely out of you,
undress you with
my eyes and
let my mind wander
over every inch
of your bare
naked soul.

Tonight there is a slow progression of
clothes coming off piece by piece.
Shadows dance across her body in
the flickering light of this candle-lit room,
I'm envious of the way they caress her skin.
She writes how she's longed for this moment,
with her tongue,
on the most sacred locations of my body.
Every profanity she draws from my lips
as she wordlessly confesses her soul,
feels like another language I had no idea I knew.

Like the Moon to Earth,
caught in continual orbit
around your center.

I want to drown in you;
to be absolutely surrounded by you,
swept away by your current,
held under by the crushing
weight of these feelings,
realizing you've taken my breath away
and I'm getting lightheaded now.
If this is the way I leave this world then
I don't know that I mind it so much.

Somehow you were able to touch me
before we ever made physical contact.
You were creeping into my heart
before you touched
my lips, my waist, my thighs.
You've consumed my soul
to the point that each beat of my pulse
says your name in a low whisper.
Now when we do touch,
it shakes me to the core in the
most exquisite of ways.

I smile each time the words
*just friends*
appear in our conversations.
I don't think that these blurred lines
are a result of my need for glasses.
Regardless, I'll be here waiting for her to
adjust her focus and clearly read the signs.

Whisper in my ear
all the ways you love me
so when a storms rages
in my mind, I can be brave.

There has been a sound struggling
to escape my lips for
quite a long time now;
it's the pounding of my heart
trying to scream out your name
with each beat.

I met you so long ago,
we kissed until nightfall,
by midnight you had
my body and my heart
and from that moment on
you became my sunrise.

A drink or two relaxes those barriers,
your walls come down ever so slightly
and some of those feelings take a chance
to run wild, free of their usual inhibitions.
Without a thought of the past that again
someone would abuse them, betray them,
or waste their precious time and effort.
I couldn't handle their trust before
but I think I'm slowly proving myself as
someone to vacation with from time to time
even though I've made my fair share of errors.

I want to discover every detail about you.
To spend the night with you would be a
dream; not for sex or physical satisfaction
but to attempt to unlock your mind. I want
to know where your thoughts go at midnight.
I want to learn about your dreams and
aspirations, what troubles you faced
in your past, who it is that has hurt you
and how I can become your security.
I want you to talk to me until all the words
become etched into my bones and I can never
let them go. My only desire is to know
every piece, every part, every poem.

When I want to feel you
on the days I can't see you.
I put all our songs on a
playlist and replay it
over & over.
By the fourth song
I can feel your touch,
by the sixth
I can taste your lips,
But I need you to know that
I wanted you here from
the moment I pressed play.

Where have you been, love?
I've been waiting my entire life
to find your gorgeous soul.

Let me lay with you
for hours at a time
and whisper sweet nothings
that mean plenty of somethings
into your ears, through your veins,
and towards your heart.

You don't always need to be strong.
Lean on me for just a second
and rest your weary bones.

I was never adventurous
until I met you,
dark places and
fear of the unknown held me back.

I was never an explorer
until I started to love you,
turning sharp corners and
lighting lanterns along
the path towards you.

I was never brave until I took that chance
to climb to the very top of your mountain.
I looked down and noticed that somehow,
you had lit up entirely with each passing day.

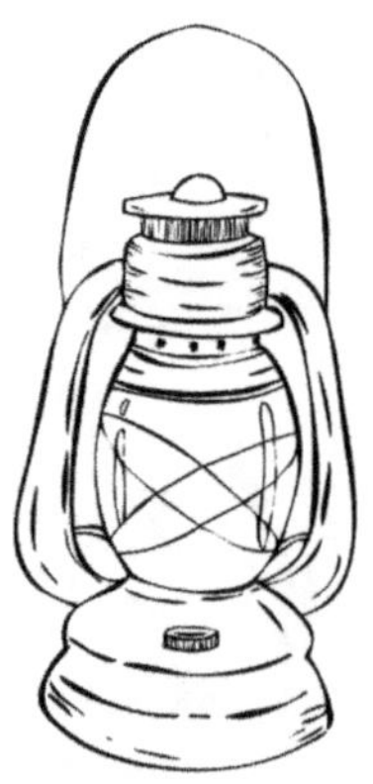

I've been with many women.
Laying in bed next to them,
my mind felt like turbulent waters
in a huge ocean; restless and dark.
But when I laid in your bed, oh,
those nights I laid in your bed
were pure tranquility.
You calmed the storm and as the
water turned crystal clear and quiet,
it was obvious to me that I should
never let something like this go.

I can't seem to stop telling
the moon and stars how
incredibly lovely she was in
the moments I make her happy.
They listen eagerly each time in
a blissful haze of naivety with me
like they haven't ever heard
another version of our story.

She is a living poem;
a haiku of patterned behavior,
coupled with stanzas of beauty,
rhymes of passion and purpose,
and an amazing approach to alliteration.
Let me pen an ode about all I've learned
and we can let this ballad flow how it goes.
I'll continue to write the verses
and enjoy her company happily.
Even if we never form a couplet,
I love the words we create together.

I've been thinking of you for hours.
The hours really seem like days.
The days feel like months
that might as well be years.
That's how long it feels that my heart
has been searching for yours.

It isn't something that needs a
name or a label or a definition.
It's really quite simple.
If it's not you, it's not anyone else.

My heart is yours.
Only you cause such an
overwhelming reaction
as it desperately tries to
break out and reach you again.
Each set of beats is a cry of
your name against my ribs.

Poets in love will forever
immortalize you in their words.
They will spill their emotions in
inked metaphors line after line,
their pens are unforgivably honest.
I don't need to carve a statue out
of marble to remember your beauty,
my goal is to write a simple book.
I want to ensure I never forget
the moments we shared, you and I,
the poet in love with the muse.

Waking at 3AM
right on the dot.
Here you are again
consuming my mind,
every single thought.
You sneak in quietly
a thief in the night,
I welcome you each time
without a fight.
I don't dream anymore
about the love I want,
instead, it's my 3AM mind
you seem to haunt.
It no longer bothers me,
I'll gladly sacrifice this sleep
as long as each lovely daydream
is a bit of hope I get to keep.

Most of these poems are
my personal love letters.
I share them with the world
in hopes that other souls
can find warmth in the words
that are meant for her.
They apply them to the ones
their own hearts ache for and
reminisce alongside me.
I will continue writing
because I know I won't lose her.
I could empty every last word from
my chest and she would still remain.

It's an addiction.
You set me on fire, oh baby,
hold me gently between your fingers,
wrap your lips around me,
inhale and exhale seductively,
until you finally stamp me out.
Each time, you light me up
and we do it again.

I know I'm not an easy person to love.
my words are almost never perfect
and I'm a continuous work in progress.
I have a hard time showing it but
I promise that this heart will
stay
right beside yours until
the day you tell it to
leave.

I'll be that old comfortable sweater you put on year after year. I'll be the soft touch of something worn and the familiar smell of faded cologne embedded in the fibers. There are a few fraying pieces and some small holes here and there but we can mend them together. I can still provide comfort and warmth whenever you need to wrap up in me. Wear me to bed and hold me close so I can touch every part of you through the night.

That feeling of comfort is slowly
making its way back through my veins,
a warmth that is so familiar,
yet, so different this time around.
It's creeping up gently like the tide
instead of an overpowering crash
of waves against the shore.
This feels solid, strong, trustworthy
like a boat on the ocean.
At the same time, it's fragile and
needs to be maintained and cared for
to ensure it stays above water.
I've been the captain of my life
for such a long time, but
I'm letting go of the wheel and
watching the sails fill with the wind.
Tossing my compass overboard,
I kick my feet up and trace
that feeling of comfort
winding its way closer and closer
to my heart.

I got to experience a
part of you that doesn't
surface unless the
conditions are right.
I know I hold a
piece of you that
most people will
never get to see.
My love,
the importance of that
doesn't go unnoticed.

3AM

My body keeps trying to
sweat her out of my system
with each nightmare but
I refuse to let her go again.

I'm not the same person you left behind anymore.
There are scars, marks, and wounds.
some old and some still healing.
Life has continued to progress
even though one hand was always
outstretched back towards you.
Timing has never been a friend of mine
but this is how the Universe works.
we love and we lose,
we fall and we rise,
we hurt and we heal.
Please forgive me for grabbing onto
every piece of you that I can,
for the Universe has never given me
a second chance at anything
in all my years of life.

Sometimes you taste like forever,
although I try to abandon those thoughts
and take off my rose-tinted glasses.
I am nothing more than a dreamer,
a lovely mess of the lies we tell ourselves
but I am content just cherishing the
ineffable way your hands feel on my skin
and seeing where we all might end up.

You are the sun and
I am the moon.
You brighten the days
as I haunt the darkness.
You are constantly whole
as I go through phases
of myself that can be seen
across the night sky.
Although we are vastly different,
I wait anxiously each day
counting the minutes until
we appear together in the sky
if only for those fleeting moments,
I'll take it.

I really want it to be us
when life settles down and
all of this has run its course.
I'd love it if we made it.

I know I don't complete you.
You aren't the type that needs to be
completed by another person.
You're perfectly fine on your own:
strong, resilient, and so sure of yourself.
But I'm not going to lie to you,
secretly I hope I'm able to fill
some of those empty spaces
that may happen to exist.

I never thought words
could have their own heartbeat
until the day you called me
*love.*

She's a raging wildfire
unlike anything you've ever seen,
burning hot and unapologetic,
filled with a swirling beauty that
can't be tamed or extinguished.
When it surrounds you
it's hard to breathe, hard to focus.
You can run for the nearest exit
or decide to trust completely that
something that beautiful
would never hurt a soul.

When you touch me
I can feel myself soften
and my entire body
seems to exhale.

The freckles you adore on my face
are little specks of Sun soaked in.
I've always loved the sunshine so
It's no wonder I carry it on my skin.
I'm also a fan of the Moon, turning those
spots into a star-filled sky, alive and free.
She caresses my cheek with her thumb
and creates constellations named after me.
Indulge in my universe endlessly dear,
whether it be sunshine or moonlight above.
You are something so magical that
even these freckles crave your love.

Tether your soul to mine.
I need something good
to keep me anchored here
with both feet on the ground.

I think I loved you the moment I saw you.
One touch and I was hooked, addicted to it all.
There's no possible way that someone
who steals all the breath from your lungs
isn't meant to mean something profound.

I handle your emotions with
spotless white gloves.
You give me your trust
and I carefully hold it close.
The things you have told me
are sorted delicately into
this locked chest of mine
and marked with FRAGILE.
There is still so much space left
for you to show me more.

There's a part of me that has been
a part of you for quite some time.
There is also a part of you still
deeply entangled in my bones.
I'm on a long journey to
figure out what that means.

I still have a long way to go but
my heart is one of the few things
already in the right place.

She is a bright spring daisy and
I am a bee bumbling nearby
waiting to land, starving for her.

I usually have no trouble
stringing together letters
of the alphabet into poetry
but this one, man this one,
she left me lost for words in
a way I'm still trying to decipher.

Everything around me had been so grey
and then you walked in one evening,
so full of color, I was awestruck.
How could anyone resist something
that incredibly beautiful.

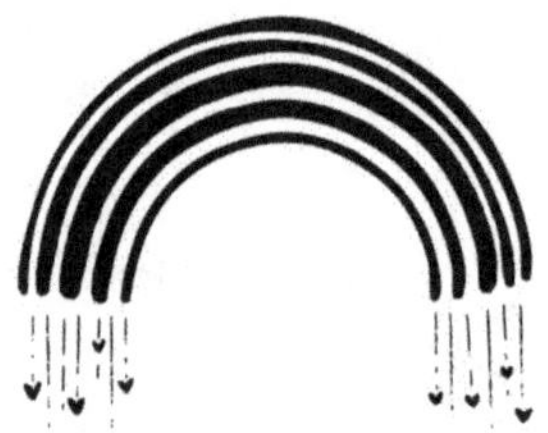

The moment I heard your laugh again
I knew I was in a world of trouble.
My heart started busting dance moves
2020 hadn't even discovered yet.

Let's just exist together.
You can go your way and I'll go mine,
but we won't do it alone.
Fall into bed with me when you
have the time to spare and I'll
hold you like the world is ending.
Let me slowly create that lasting
feeling that you will crave again,
the one that's distinctly and uniquely me.
Trust me when I say I've got you
because I don't intend on letting go,
this time I'd like to stay if you won't run.
Let's just exist together love,
and it won't mean a single thing
to anyone else but you and me.

I had so much alcohol
that night we kissed,
I haven't had a drink
that good since.

There is something here that I cannot lose
because I know deep in my heart
that I won't find it anywhere else.
There are little moments, memories,
and feelings that can only be described
as irreplaceable.

You have all of me,
until the sun sets for the last time
and the stars fail to appear.

You say my name in a way
I have never heard before
and it is like music to my ears
even though you didn't sing a note.

I could get so completely lost in
your eyes if I let myself.
You'd pull me in close with a look
and wrap yourself around me.
I'd shake hands with that familiar
feeling, that warmth creeping into
all the cracks I've been trying to mend.
I think I might want to be lost again,
I tear up the map I've held for so long
and embrace this existence.
Let's get lost and never found because,
simply put, your lips on mine and
our hearts dancing together is
what I desire most.

Loving you is like the ocean.
I could sit quietly and enjoy
the view for hours on end.
It has moments of ebb and flow
but the current keeps me steady,
floating towards our destination.

My hands are made to
hold, caress, touch, and feel.
Very rarely have they encountered
someone that touched back
in quite the way you have.

She's like a good book
I don't want to put down.
I'm dying to read her
cover to cover.

I will always care for you,
probably too much,
even if we aren't together,
even if we stop talking one day,
and even if the distance is too great.
That kind of feeling in your soul is
not one that is easily
or maybe ever forgotten,
you still have me.

It's July 4th
but none of these fireworks
shine as bright as you do.

Your name is still
the most precious thing
to have danced across my lips.

As we navigate this path together
I'll take your hand and wonder
If you think there's room for me to
beat within your heart again.

Tell me more about your love,
how you managed to bury it
so deeply within my bones that
when I am with you the
rhythm of my heart changes.
How it seems to have made a
home here in my chest and
weakens the remainder of my resolve.
And how it takes my breath away
each and every time you offer
a little part of your heart up to me.

I've grown to cherish
those little black hearts you send,
but I feel the need to tell you
they should be red.
A vibrant red like roses
that have started to bloom
deep within the dormant parts of my soul.
A dark, dusky red
like the towering brick walls
we're slowly knocking out of our way.
A hazy red like sunset, a metaphor
for closing one chapter and starting anew.
A flickering, burning red like a campfire
and the warmth we feel when our hands brush.
Shades of red like the autumn leaves
that fall and, much like how
I've fallen for you, they're unable
to stop and pick themselves back up.

I have so much of her in my heart
some days it feels like it may burst.
I know that I want all of her,
the good and the bad,
the tears and the kisses,
the arm around my body at 2AM,
misunderstandings and forgiveness.
I can handle every piece gently.

She looked at my body like it
was a work of art,
like the Mona Lisa or
The Sistine Chapel.
She studied me like
a blank notebook and
all I wanted
was for her to paint
her soul onto my pages.

My name seems to taste different on your
lips now, sweet, desirable,
and maybe even irresistible.
The way it dances across your tongue
making sound waves ripple through my
chest is something so uniquely you.
When you call my name, it seems to echo
through the room like a beautiful
melody. I want to record it just in case
you change your mind.

You taste like new beginnings and
a lifetime of memories all at once,
as if the Universe brought us together
once more from some other time and place.
I found you again at last.

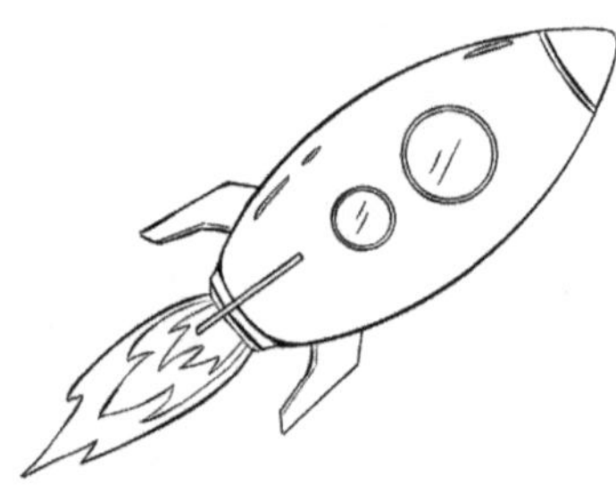

My favorite feeling is when a person does
something and your immediate,
overwhelming thought is "I love you."
It could be something small or stupid or
very typical of them, but they do it and
your brain is just like, yeah, that right
there is why I love this human.

She makes my mind
a little hazy but
these feelings are
crystal clear.

Come away with me and,
under the cover of night,
I promise to hold you close
and just listen.

Be patient if you notice me studying you,
for I am creating a map simply entitled Her.
It contains the contours of your body and
the secrets you've shared late at night.
It whispers of gentle touches, slow kisses
and passionate embraces.
It lays out the path from me to you and
you to me, to ensure we never get lost again.
An X marks the spot that I ignite within you,
the long-lost feelings that have awakened
are a compass guiding you home to me.
When it's finally complete,
I'll take it to the grave.
I don't dare risk anyone discovering the rare
and beautiful treasure I've stumbled upon.

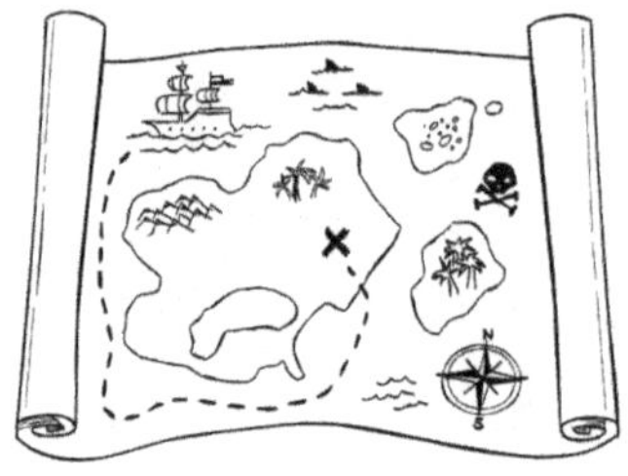

A familiar voice lures me out into the
surf and suddenly the undertow sweeps
me off my feet. It draws me away from the
safety of shore and everything I have
known so far, out into the blue and the
embrace of your arms. I'm treading water
and contemplating this change; it feels
remarkable to be surrounded by the warmth
from all sides instead of wandering the
vast emptiness of a typical shoreline.

I've always wished on falling stars,
never thinking we may have
something in common until I started
                falling,
                        falling,
                                falling
                                    for you.

You embraced me and,
despite my rough edges,
I fell right into your soul
and fit perfectly.

I looked at you and really saw you
and I know you realized that much,
but I don't think you ever understood
all of the beauty and wonder you contain.

Pay close attention to
the songs I send you,
they say all the feelings
I cannot find words for.

I want to
write poems
across her body
with my fingertips.

You can't lie to your soul
for it has seen many lifetimes.
It remembers the touch,
the taste, the feel
of the one you're destined for.
Try as you may to deny it,
there's no escaping the gravity of fate.

Simply put,
I lack the vocabulary to describe you,
no adjective could possibly be enough.
What I can tell you though is that,
for me, you've made love a verb.

Your smile
warms
my heart
the way
no fire
ever could.

I want to be your home,
where you come to rest after
a long day at work.
I want to be your calm, your security,
your sigh of relief when you see me.
The place you lay your head at night
and unload the day,
that's what I want to be.
Hang your heart next to mine
on the coat rack, my love,
and take a chance on me.

Let me be your permanent
in this world full of temporary.
We'll figure it out together
because I'm still hoping that
we can make this all work.

Sing my insecurities a lullaby.
Put them to bed after
years of sleepless nights.
I can finally be myself
without holding back because
your song has set me free.

A dark room
Two souls collide
Eye contact
Soft music
And
Slow, passionate love.

It was you before I ever decided.
Something like celestial magic,
immediately strong can't hide it,
like how the stars can't help but shine.
I tried to explain it the best I could.

I want to love you in every language
so that there is never a chance you
misunderstand my feelings for you.

She provokes a different part of my soul.

I finally discovered the words to describe why this is so special, why this love is so intoxicating. My heart has overflowed many times, but my soul has never been touched. There is a deeper connection formed when someone moves past your heart and finds a way to explore your soul, giving it a gentle embrace for the first time. There is a burst of color, of clarity, of something even you didn't know existed. It's not better than what exists already, but it's so different that you can't seem to catch your breath at times. There is a person that understands every square inch of my heart… my person, and suddenly, there exists a person that my entire being is telling me feels so remarkably familiar from long ago.
Maybe it doesn't need a full explanation, something so moving and mysterious, but I don't want this to just be a singular moment in time. I want this kind of love to be a lifetime.

I will continue to make
memories with you
for as long as you'll
allow me the pleasure.

The world spins around us
at an incredible speed.
You and I are in the eye
of the storm; calm,
still, and eerily quiet.
Close your eyes,
shut off your mind,
and just see me
with your heart.

As turned on as I always am,
I have no interest in sex
without a deeper connection.
I need to see what your eyes convey
in the moment of this collision.
I want to move in sync with
your heartbeat as I slowly
let my walls crumble around us.
I'll take a deep breath and kiss you,
transferring the trust I rarely give out.
I refuse to share myself with
anyone less than a true lover.

*Beauty is in the eye of the beholder.*
So next time all is quiet and
there are no distractions,
really take the time to
*behold her.*

Nestled inside your warm embrace I think, if
someone asked me what my definition of love
is, this is what I will say. It is a smile
that freezes time, a voice that becomes your
favorite sound, the soft feeling of her skin
against yours, the electricity of your lips
meeting like it's the first time each time.
It is when the fierceness of her touch is
balanced by the tenderness of her heart.
It is drowning in the scent of her neck,
tracing the scars of the past across her
back, and navigating these heavy seas of
emotion. At this point she has made a home
within you, such a commanding presence, yet
so vulnerable and unaware of her worth.
You'll want to show her happiness like she's
never experienced. When they ask about this
love, I will tell them how your whispered
words have infiltrated my existence, how
you've crept into the deepest parts of my
soul and dared to stay, and that somehow,
you've silently gotten past the fence I've
built around my tired heart. My mind insists
that I don't deserve this kind of love, her
love, but at night I silently pray to the
stars not to take this away.
I want to embed these words into each person
that asks what love is.
     I'll tell them that love, is her.

We discovered a frequency
that nobody else could hear,
a wavelength of deep
communication all our own.
And I fell for you so fast then
that the Universe must
have already had this planned.

The night sky and your soul
both shone bright with wonder.
They brought me peace, calm,
and so much to ponder.

The beauty of the snow
that fell overnight
is still no match for yours.
Besides, I'm falling harder
than it ever could.

You make me happier than
I ever thought I could be.
I'll spend the rest of my life
making sure you always
know that I mean it.

If I had a flower for every time
I've thought of you this past month,
I'd have a garden overflowing with
so much unconfined beauty that
even the honeybees would buzz about it
for seasons to come.

I didn't know it could be so
goddamn beautiful
for bodies to move as one
until last night;
flawless acts of perfection.

I think my heart
will always do
a little
"!"
with that jolt of
e l e c t r i c i t y
when it sees you.

I've found something that
quiets my anxiety better
than alcohol ever could.

You.

I love you from
sunrise to sunset,
once a heart feels this
it doesn't ever forget.

We went together as well as the words
scrawled across the pages of my notebook.
An effortless translation of emotion,
poetry of the bodies.

I never liked cigarettes until
I inhaled them with your kiss.
That's all it took to get
completely addicted to you.

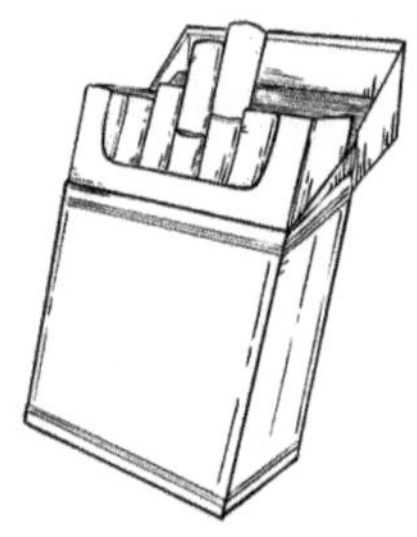

I want to spend
all night learning
every intimate little
sound you make.

You and I
speak the same language,
there has never been
a need to translate our souls.
You were made for
far better things my love,
and I'm right here
waiting to show you.

Your smile manages to erase
every thought in my mind.
What a wonderful weapon
for one to possess.

You permeate my every thought,
my every sense, my every moment.
Not anything specific about you,
but just **you** are powerful enough
to carve your name into every surface
that exists inside this lovesick soul.

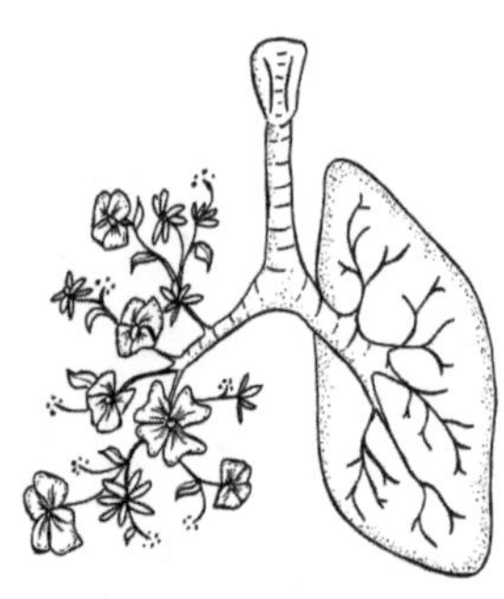

The darkness inside
seems to get
a little bit brighter
every time she calls me
*baby.*

There are over 170,000 words
in current use in the English language.
Yet, there isn't a single one that
can accurately describe the
compelling complexities and
breathtaking beauty of
the person that you are.

Lay with me through Summer's last breath
under the canopies of bronzing foliage.
In a tent by the fireside, you and I share
whiskey kisses at Autumn's appearance.
Be still my racing heart, for it has found
heaven on the tip of your tongue and
longs to bask in this feeling a bit longer.
I never tire of thinking about you
or having your soul tied to mine,
as you are the same in every season.
Spring, Summer, Fall, Winter,
you are perfect for me.

I want to surround myself with your
heartbeat; to have the sound vibrate my body
like the front row of a rock concert, to
have each set of beats echo so loud inside
my head that I hear nothing else.
Bum-Bum     Bum-Bum    Bum-Bum
I want to move with you to the rhythm as it
quickens, intensifies, and becomes erratic
when our bodies get closer… closer and
finally meet as we do this dance.

I want to be surrounded by all of you.

I do not operate the same in love.
My heart is the impulsive leader
that the rest of me blindly follows.
There is no room for thought
when it comes to loving you,
my mind fades away softly.
I choose to trust feelings and,
almost like a metal detector,
I follow the increasing rate of
my pulse as I get closer to you.
Thoughts can control feelings,
sometimes in a positive way, but
I can't seem to set limits for this love.
From my head to my heart and
my soul to my bones, I am yours.

Call me an addict
because I can't seem to
ditch this hunger.
Snaking through my veins
is a craving I'm learning
to keep under control.
I'm an addict with a pen
instead of a needle,
overflowing with words.
The only relief from these
withdrawals is to let some
of my thoughts spill out
because I can't take a hit of
*her*
everyday.

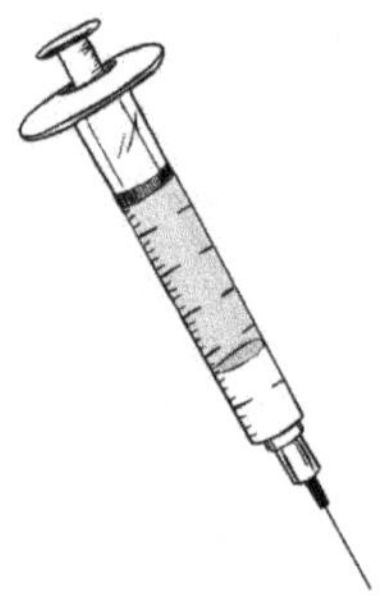

I'll gladly drown in the
waves that you cause
because I've always
been a fan of the water.

Lay me down in the darkness,
set fire to the candles the way
you have ignited my soul.
Take your sweet time because
I've got all the time or
we can pretend that the
concept doesn't even exist.
Conquer me like a long hike,
slow down and observe,
explore every trail,
wander every pathway,
until, at the top, I peak.
We can come back down
together and start again.

I don't think you'll ever not
evoke these feelings within me.
You could break my heart time
after time and it would still choose
to come back to you;
beaten, bruised, and patched
back up again ready for more.

The sky is pink this evening and it
reminds me of the blush of her cheeks
in the moments we acknowledge
with words, feelings we both try to bury.
Our insides dance to beating hearts
and the butterflies are frantic with escape,
but outwardly, just being people that
enjoy each other's company has
been the most spectacular part.

It was merely a whisper over
the noise of the evening
when she said,
*"I want to make love to you."*

I'm just a wildflower that somehow
ended up in a garden of roses,
trying to grow towards the sun
while dodging the protruding thorns.
My only goal is to bloom but
I know that these things take time.

Her hands caress my body
underneath my shirt,
usually I'm a little insecure
but I couldn't care less tonight.
I want to savor the high of her kiss
and I pray my knees don't buckle
under the weight of these emotions.

Tattooed on my skin
A metaphor of us both
And our journey here
A lesson to keep
Two different people like
Mountains and the sea

When the days are long
and your soul is weary,
take comfort in my words
and find shelter within me.

You're my mountain;
the hardest climb I've ever made
but so beautiful at the top.
I'm your ocean;
difficult to navigate at times
but tranquil and true in the end.

My love for you is endless like the ocean.

We have a wildfire burning between us,
but you keep throwing water on the flames.
Why am I the only one willing to get
swept up in this raging inferno,
confident that we won't get burned?

I was never a believer in religion
until the thrill of her touch
brought me to my knees and
I started to pray for more.
I swear to god I'd ditch this
devil on my shoulder if it meant
she would hold me and lay
kisses across my back again.
The electricity she leaves behind
is so sacred that space and time
lose all meaning.
I'll confess that my thoughts
may be unholy at times but
I'd be content just singing hymns
of her every night instead.

I fall to pieces at your touch
and never want to put
myself back together.

I would love to paint
a spectacular life
onto your canvas.

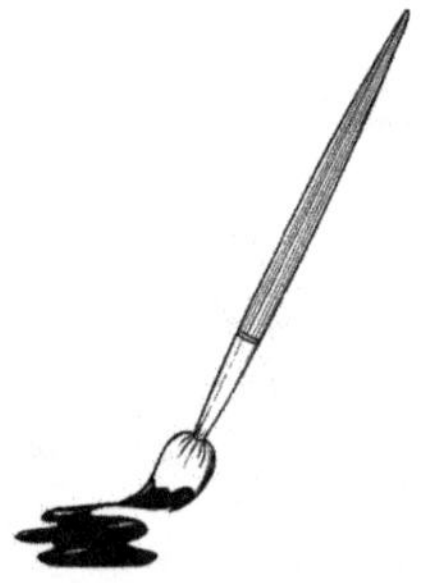

You don't have to say a word
to let me know what you're feeling.
We are one in the same,
you have touched my soul
many more times than my body
and left your unique mark there.

In orbit around one another,
a moon belonging to its planet.
A connected constellation
like the connection our
celestial bodies made
over and over that night.

You caught me
at my weakest
but even at my
strongest I would
still fall for you.

I can see adventure all around me
and I'm dying to find where I might fit.
I'm longing to discover something new
to reward my growth and change,
to expand and try new things without fear.
I want to fall in love with life again
in the same fashion I've fallen for you,
intensely and without reservation.

Breathing heavy,
moving slow,
hands wander,
eyes closed.
Get completely lost in me.

She is a masterpiece,
the Starry Night of Van Gogh
swirls across my vision
when she walks by.
Every interaction leads to
emotion colorfully splattered
across my Jackson Pollock heart.
Even a museum doesn't deserve
something as exquisite as her.

All I needed was another
taste of your lips and
I became a master of words.
You made me a poet.

I cherish the moments when
you reach out for me,
when small bits of emotion
spill out from your cracks.
You say what you feel and
it is a spectacular rarity,
memorable like Halley's Comet.
I'm a sucker for your words
and even more, your affection.

There is a peace I find with you
in moments like silently lying in bed
listening to our breathing, legs overlapped.
I feel it in the way you do small things
out of love like lightly run your finger
from my forehead to the tip of my nose.
I didn't know I needed you, but I still do.

You are always heavy on my mind,
or maybe it's inside my body, both.
Your words weave in and out of my ribcage
and are wound around my spine, each vertebrae
a tangled mess of missing you and loving you.
I am ensnared in this web of no escape
and I'm more than happy to accept my fate.

I search within for my meaning
and you are both there,
names embroidered on my lungs
so I can't help but breathe you in.
Such important pieces of my existence.

Your sweet words, slow kisses,
memories of your hands roaming,
and the fingerprints left on my heart.
We could end this thing and
never speak to one another again
and I'd still have you all over me.

She walked in the door and
I didn't stand a chance.
She kissed my lips and
my heart started to dance.

You are the teacher and
I want to be your student.
Please, teach me how to love you
the way you want to be loved.

We're stranded on this planet
with millions of people but
the only soul I search for
in every life, is yours.

You give me that strange feeling
of floating through space, yet
it's so familiar, I feel it in my memories.
Maybe we have been here before
with constellations hidden in our souls,
you and I a part of Ursa Minor except
these feelings are anything but minor.

My heart overflows out
of my chest and all I know
is that I continue to love you.
My resolve unravels in
the midnight hours and
you flood my every thought.

Paint me with the colors of a
love that is tried and true.
Believe me, when my heart beats,
the skip in that rhythm is for you.

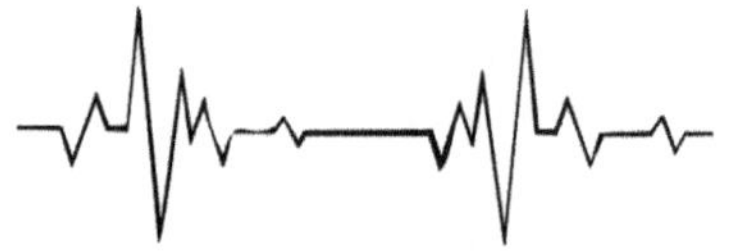

Let me show you what love is,
feel it surging through my embrace.
There is the heat of our bodies and
a spark that makes our hearts race.
We liked the darkness of rooms
with only flickering candles for light.
A metaphor for how you lit up my soul,
a flame in the dark that burned just right.

I don't want to forget
all the secrets that
our bodies have shared.

Hold me like the night sky
embraces the moon and
wrap me in your stars.

I loved you in the rain, but it isn't
always soft and sweet like the poets say.
We were an unpredictable thunderstorm, her
and I, gradually yet intensely building.
Energy discharged,
a rapid flash of light
streaked across the sky,
target acquired and a
direct hit to my core.
I didn't think it was possible for
lightning to strike twice but there I was,
electricity crackling all over my skin and
the spark of another love awakening inside.

I want our bodies
to say more than
our mouths tonight.
Talk to me with your hands,
let your fingers trace
an adventure down my back
and take me on a journey
somewhere far away.

My heart and my soul
have always been my
trusted guides in
this journey through life.
So when they dropped me
on my ass in front of you,
I went for it with every bit
of love I had left in me.

When I bite my lip
come climb onto my lap
and take my face in both hands.
Kiss me deeply and grind
your hips into me, teasing.
That's how I want your love.
Confident and carefree.

You didn't just knock
on the door to my heart,
you kicked that shit in
unannounced and urgent
as if you were rescuing me
from a burning building.
My chest has been on
fire since that moment.

This thing between us started as
a small ripple on the surface of a lake.
It has evolved over the years into
white caps on choppy ocean waves.
It might just be me, but it feels now
as though a tsunami of this love could
knock me off my feet at any moment,
if we are ever brave enough to release it.

I can find pieces of us
in every song I listen to.
As the music fills my head,
all I'm ever left with is an
untamed wildfire burning
our story deep into my soul.

Cling to me in the dark
because not all nights
have stars that appear,
I still need your light.

I had planned to seduce you
with an alluring performance
but as our eyes met in the crowd
I was overtaken by your spell.
You captivated my attention, love,
enchanted me with mystical movements,
and hypnotized me with a whisper.
I'm mesmerized by this illusion
and haven't managed to break free.
I am no longer a lone magician,
we have formed this power of
irresistible attraction together.

You've called it magic.

There is something about you
that sets my insides ablaze and
reduces my self-control to ash.

We come together intensely,
full of natural wild and I'm
no longer scared of the
explosive thunder we create.
The kind that goes
from a low rumbling to
a deafening roar in an instant.
Continue with me and witness
all the storms we can weather.

It may not be
something official,
but I am yours
where matters of
the heart are concerned.

I want to carve our initials
into the bark of a tree
and watch how we
    grow
        and grow
            and grow.

I'm in love with
our *impossibility*
and how we keep
coming back for more.
I'm in love with you
and how it feels to
have your love in return.

Allow me to seduce your
empty and broken heart.
I'll flick on the lights after
years of darkness and
start polishing surfaces.
Let me light a fire in the hearth
and warm you from the inside.
Take my outstretched hand
and come alive again with me.

We had galaxies between the two of us,
the black holes in my heart produced
an Earth sized ache for you.
Our love seems to show up and disappear,
much like the lunar waxing and waning,
and you want me again to be
the loyal Callisto to your Jupiter.
So, I'm throwing this love into the void
and seeing what course it charts
across the Milky Way.
It's in the arms of the Universe now
and officially out of my hands.

You don't just cross my mind,
you've pitched a tent there
and haven't left in months.
The fire you've built is steady
and, under a star-studded night,
is the beacon I follow back to you.
I used to come and go but I became
homesick for you when I'd leave.
Homesick for you when I went home.
A new horizon is approaching and I'm
hoping you'll watch the sunrise with me.

My late-night thoughts
and hazy daydreams
are all full of you.

You are the strongest drug to
ever circulate my system.
Even now I feel you coursing
through my veins as if you were
always meant to be there,
an inevitable part of me
back where it belongs.

I ache to be your
constant lover,
not an occasional
connection.

Meet me in my dreams tonight
where things are simple and clear.
We can get lost in each other
without interruption or fear.

There's so much I
want to say to you,
so many words on
the tip of my tongue.
I wonder if you can
taste them when we kiss.

She causes a heat to
move through my body
when our eyes meet
creating a full body blush,
a rose-colored tint only hers.

You touch me tenderly like I
am everything you dreamed of.
With your hands on me, I would bet
my life on this connection lasting.
This is the gravity of what you do
and I long to be with you, always.

When the space between
our bodies disappears,
we drink each other in.
She is soft like whiskey and
has the same burn of desire.
Our kisses get as reckless
as our hearts in this moment.
Covered in shameless passion,
you swallow me in pieces but
all I need to live is a taste of you.

You glow like moonlight
when we're together and
I see stars when you smile.
You are an entire world of lovely.

A 52-card deck
and I draw the Joker,
what are the odds that the
Queen of Hearts would
jest with someone like me.

Showing you my raw poetry,
these words, this alphabetic art,
is me trusting you completely
with my unpolished heart.

She made my body smile
with the touch of her hand
and caused a symphony
inside my chest with a kiss.

I forget how to breathe
each time she touches my skin
and the rhythm of my heart skips
when she whispers our sins.
Her lips lay kisses down my body
like she's following a map,
coming back for treasure she buried
years ago, knowing I contain no traps.
Three words softly exchanged
back and forth all night and
I wish I could just tell her that
nothing has ever felt this right.
One or both, love or lust,
whatever I feel I know I must
keep control and take it slow
so she doesn't decide to let me go.

I'm looking through my telescope
at the planets and stars, all the while
realizing that you are the only heavenly body
that really matters in this vast universe.

I'm balancing on the ledge
with my heart wide open.
It is here I will wait for you
with hope in my daydreams,
because in these dreams
it's always you.

It's pouring outside and I'm lost in thought
about this love between us that grew.
This summer rain and I are both falling fast,
completely head over heels for you.

I wish I could love in moderation,
but my heart doesn't know how to.
It only knows intense, headfirst love
especially when it comes to loving you.

You are forever the wild fury made
to balance my quiet innocence.
This is why we both devour
each other with hungry hearts
time after time without hesitation.

I'm ready to love you
with no strings attached
if that's what you have to offer.
You are worth it and I can still dream.

Your love is a honeysuckle vine
and I've become so tangled up,
mesmerized by how tantalizingly
sweet you taste on my lips.

You, who opened suns in my heart, have become just that as well, my sun. I'm mesmerized by your fiery spirit and the warmth you cause within me. Drawn in by your magnetic field, I lay claim to my chosen path revolving around you. I have been blinded by your light and now I will dance like a runaway flame on your surface until we burn out.

I want a cabin on a mountainside
or a cute cottage on a lake with you.
You would wake up to coffee and
the smell of things I had baked.
We could have a tent in the woods,
even bathing in a creek would be fine.
To be honest, anywhere we end up,
you and me, would be absolutely divine.

I'm surrounded by
all of these hearts,
but apparently
the only one I've been
chasing for nine years now,
has been yours.

She loves me, she loves me not.
The flower petals fall like autumn leaves
floating with the wind towards
fragile, unknown destinations.
The stem, now bare like our bodies,
contained all the reasons you could
never be mine and I, never yours.
I turned it into a blank slate and
am watching these new blossoms of
love slowly grow just for her and I.

You taught me what my heart is for
when you showed me yours that night.
You've wrapped yourself around my soul,
your grasp on me is gentle but tight.
You give me feelings that I can't ignore
as your whispered words consume my mind.
There's something uniquely you inside me
as if the stars made way for us
as they aligned.
Every day, every night, every hour I am
discovering new parts of you,
all I want is more.
I can't seem to anchor my heart when
I think of you, it takes flight and soars.

*You have touched my soul differently.*

I wish you could overhear
the way I talk about you,
as if you were the oxygen
in my lungs and the
blood in my veins.

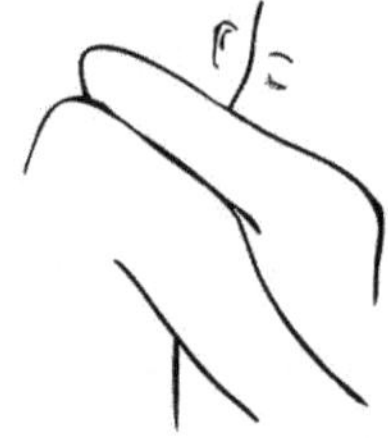

I've witnessed the colors you display,
every light shade of lavender and
yellows and oranges in every hue.
Now sunsets and flowers don't look
the same because the most beautiful
array of color for me, is you.

You may not be able to see them yet
but there are flowers peacefully
blooming within your heart again.
They are growing, feeding on us,
and coming alive more with each day.

We take the plunge and
dive into this headfirst.
There is nothing caging
these feelings anymore.
You have undressed me,
left me naked out here
skinny dipping with you.

I'm beginning to see why Da Vinci dedicated
so much of his time to studying and
sketching hands, because I want to do the
same. Your hands hold so much power over
me, they are mysterious in so many ways. I
want to know how your fingertips send
electricity into my skin when they graze my
hips. When your hand holds mine, it feels
like the last piece of a puzzle
fitting perfectly in place. Your hands all
over my body is not an uncomfortable
insecurity like others, I crave your touch.
Your hands, outside and inside of me, have
reawakened a fire that I didn't know I was
missing. The touch of your hands makes me
come alive.

Hold me close in
those fragile moments
after love is made.
I'm not ready for our
bodies to go their
separate ways.

Don't forget to breathe
as you explore all of me
until the sun kisses our
skin through the window.

You don't cross my mind,
you've lived there quite a while.
You're my sunrise and my sunset,
all those little moments I can't forget.
My rainy days and blue skies,
and I can see it in your eyes.
You feel the same overwhelming bliss,
full of endless possibilities when we kiss.

My heart will find no peace
until you and I become us.
You have planted seeds in
my soul that have been
growing like passion fruit vines,
overtaking all they encounter.

She whispers softly in my ear
and my mind coupled with her touch
causes my body to  r e a c t.
I'm dying to move her along but
I don't want this to end any sooner.
Teasing and taunting with kisses,
I can't help but grit my teeth.
She gets to the point and I can feel
her smile as my body sighs in relief
and a low moan escapes my lips.
Her skin on mine acts as blank pages
and the love we make is poetry
written over and over in the night.

This heart in my chest is
brimming with love for you,
overflowing like a creek bed
after heavy spring rain.
Rapids form in one area, yet
calm around the next bend,
much like you and me.

The past isn't for me anymore,
the future is looking forward
to my arrival very soon.
I hope it confirms that a love
like this will be worth the wait.

We see fragments of each other
in the world around us and can't
help but share those moments.
We exchange songs that speak the
words we're not ready to commit to and
share our wants disguised as daydreams.
We carry one another in the back of
our minds and we know that love
is too weak a word for what we feel.

I like it when you love me,
when you're comfortable
enough to let words escape.
Our love is a reservoir of
lessons learned on both sides
and, as it has grown, so have we.

If you keep me wild,
I promise to keep you safe.
If you keep me down to earth,
I'll keep you searching for more.
You balance out my overabundance
of caution with your adventurous spirit.
I provide a safety net for your emotions
and a gentle hand to hold yours as
the other caresses your beautiful heart.
We set each other free in all the
ways we're both used to holding back.
Show me the way we can live life,
build anew after all our mistakes,
and I assure you that I will protect
all of your vulnerable parts.

The most intimate thing we
can do is let someone in,
reveal our heart and soul,
and trust them to hold
onto each one tenderly.
Have faith in me.

Your hands find mine in the dark
and I ponder all the different ways
I can hold them and never let go.
They run up and down my body,
fingers lightly caressing my skin and
I want to know how to give you
more and more of me each time.
You have me covered in emotion
like a weighted blanket, but I really
just want to swim in it all with you
without limitations or fear.
I keep you in the quiet part of me
like the quiet that ensues after
a summer rainstorm, peaceful
as this candlelit room.

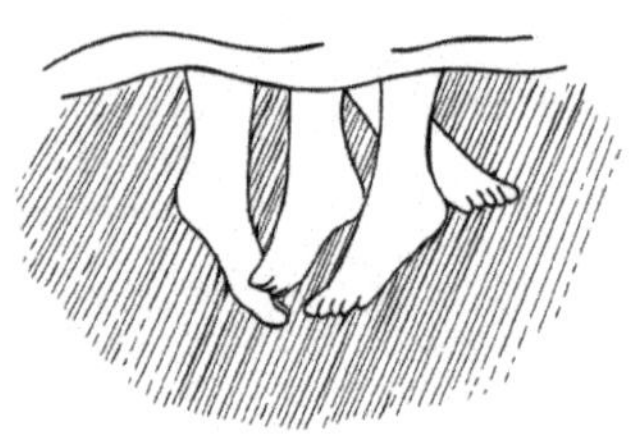

Dripping with desire
at the details we discuss,
this is how I spend my nights
having conversations with lust.

I want you to experience a
soft love with someone who
can carry your heart's trust.
Someone who takes the time.
Someone like me.